Shortcuts SAMPLER

by Roxanne Carter

That Patchwork Place®

ACKNOWLEDGMENTS

I would like to thank my husband and best friend, Rob, for his patience and understanding; Mary Hickey and Jaqui Betts for their help; everyone at That Patchwork Place for their encouragement; and especially my students who taught me so much. It would have been impossible to write this book without them.

CREDITS

Editor ....Barbara Weiland
Copy Editor ....Liz McGehee
Text and Layout Design ....Shea Dutton
Cover Design ....Judy Petry
Photography ....Brent Kane
Illustration and Graphics .... Joanne Lauterjung

Shortcuts Sampler©
© 1993 by Roxanne Carter

That Patchwork Place, Inc.
PO Box 118, Bothell, WA 98041-0118 USA

Printed in the United States of America
98 97 96 95 94 93   6 5 4 3 2 1

Carter, Roxanne,
      Shortcuts sampler / Roxanne Carter.
           p.   cm.
      ISBN 1-56477-023-0 :
      1. Patchwork—Patterns.   2. Quilting—Patterns.   I. Title.
      TT835.C39   1993
      746.9'7—dc20   92-40607
                                                              CIP

CONTENTS

Introduction 4
Shortcuts Sampler 5
    Blocks
        Rolling Stone 6
        Snowball 7
        Jenny's Block 8
        Union Square 9
        Card Trick 10
        Evening Star 11
        Land of the Midnight Sun 12
        Castles in the Air 13
        Roman Strip 14
        Fifty-Four Forty or Fight 15
        Morning Star 16
        Star of the East 17
    How to Construct an Eight-Pointed (Le Moyne) Star 18
    Setting the Blocks 19
    Quilt Top Assembly 19
    Borders 19
    Quilt Finishing 19
    Templates 20

INTRODUCTION

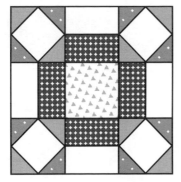

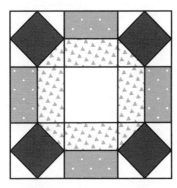

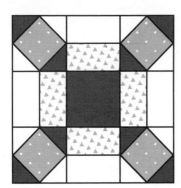

Learning new techniques and shortcuts is always fun, but it is even more exciting when you create a new project at the same time. Shortcuts Sampler was designed to help you gain new skills while you put together a beautiful quilt.

In *Shortcuts: A Concise Guide to Rotary Cutting*, Donna Lynn Thomas provides instructions for rotary cutting a wide variety of commonly used patchwork shapes without using templates. The twelve 12" blocks included in *Shortcuts Sampler* are made using all of the great timesaving methods featured in Donna's book. Combined with the lattices, pieced cornerstones, and a border, the blocks will make a quilt 60" x 76". You can make a larger quilt by using some of the block patterns more than once and changing the color placement so they look different. Study carefully the photos on the back cover to see what an intriguing difference color placement can make in the final appearance of each block and the entire quilt. The blocks to the left also show how different fabric color placements can change the look of a block.

Fabric numbers in the individual block instructions simply indicate the number of different fabrics needed, to make that particular section of the block.

Each sampler block is shown on a grid in which one square is equal to 1". By examining the grid and counting the number of squares in a block, you can easily see its size. To determine the cut size of squares and rectangles, you simply add ½" to both the width and height of the finished size.

Triangles, diamonds, trapezoids, chevrons, and hexagons require adding slightly different seam allowances to determine the cut size. For example, in *Shortcuts*, Donna Thomas explains that to compute the cut size of a half-square triangle, you must determine the finished size of the short, on-grain side of the triangle and add ⅞". This gives you the size of the square to cut. When you cut this square in half, the resulting half-square triangle will be the correct size.

¼" | Finished Size | ¼"

¼" + ¼" = ½"

For your convenience, the correct cutting measurements are included in the directions for each sampler block so you won't need to do any calculations. (All cutting measurements include ¼"-wide seam allowances.) It is important to use an accurate ¼" guide on your machine to stitch all seams.

With the knowledge you gain from making these blocks, you will be able to rotary cut any piece of any block as long as you know the finished size of the piece.

The yardage requirements provided below are based on 44"- wide fabrics that have been prewashed and have a usable width of 42". You will have fabric left over to save for other sampler or scrap quilts.

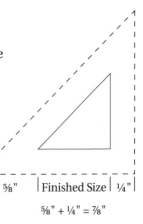

⅝" | Finished Size | ¼"

⅝" + ¼" = ⅞"

All page references in the block directions refer to the basic strip-piecing and rotary-cutting techniques in *Shortcuts*. If you are unfamiliar with these techniques, you will want to obtain a copy of the book.

SHORTCUTS SAMPLER

Finished Size: 60" x 76"
Materials: 44"-wide fabric

Choose fabrics that you love and that work together. For easy identification, the quilt blocks shown here have been shaded to match my quilt shown on the front cover. I suggest you place tracing paper over each block and color it to match your fabric colors. You might want to make several tracings of each block so you can try a variety of color arrangements before selecting the one you will use for your quilt. Then use your colored tracing as a guide as you cut and piece each block.

Blocks and Background
1 yd. each of 4 different fabrics
1½ yds. background fabric
Sashing
1 yd. background or color used for center of strip-pieced lattice
1½ yds. dark fabric (a solid works best)
¼ yd. contrasting fabric for cornerstones

Border
2½ yds. light print or solid-colored fabric for borders cut along the lengthwise grain. (If you wish to cut the borders across the width of the fabric, you will need only 1 yard.)
Backing
3½ yds. fabric of your choice
Binding
¾ yd. fabric of your choice

ROLLING STONE

Make the Rolling Stone Block to learn how to make a boxed square and how to strip piece the side units. Refer to *Shortcuts*, pages 12 and 13.

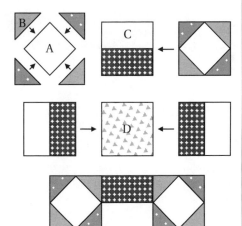

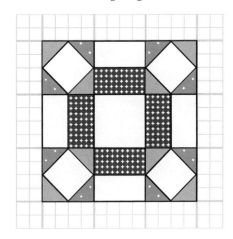

Piecing Diagram

Rolling Stone Block

Corner Units: Pieces A and B

1. Piece A: Cut 4 squares, each 3⅜" x 3⅜".
2. Piece B: Cut 8 squares, each 2⅞" x 2⅞". Stack the squares and cut once diagonally to yield 16 half-square triangles.

3. Sew 2 triangles (B) to opposite corners of square (A). Repeat with the remaining 2 triangles for each block. It helps to nub the corners of the triangles before stitching them to the squares (*Shortcuts*, page 21). Make 4.

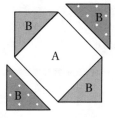

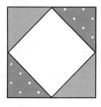

Side Units: Piece C

1. Cut 1 strip, 2½" x 22", from Fabric #1 and 1 strip from Fabric #2.
2. With raw edges matching and right sides together, stitch strips together ¼" from one long edge. Press seam toward the darker fabric. Cut the strip-pieced unit into 4 segments, each 4½" wide.

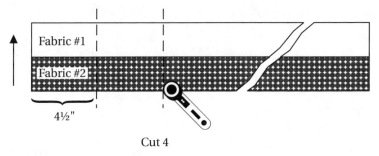

Cut 4

Center Unit: Piece D

1. Cut 1 square, 4½" x 4½".

Block Assembly

1. Arrange units as shown in the piecing diagram.
2. Sew the units together in horizontal rows.
3. Sew rows together to complete the block.

SNOWBALL

Make the Snowball Block to learn how to strip piece the Ninepatch unit and how to trim the corners from a large square to create the Snowball unit. Refer to *Shortcuts,* pages 23 and 24.

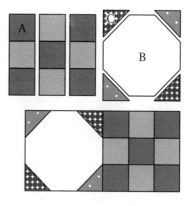

Ninepatch Unit: Piece A

1. Cut 3 strips, each 2½" x 12", from Fabric #1; cut 3 strips from Fabric #2.
2. Sew the strip-pieced units as shown. From the first strip-pieced unit, cut 4 segments, each 2½" wide.   Cut 2 segments, each 2½" wide, from the second strip-pieced unit.

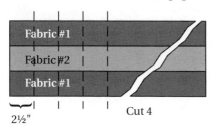
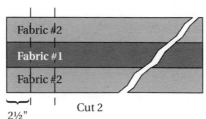

3. Assemble 2 Ninepatch units as shown.

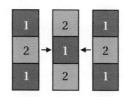

Ninepatch Unit

Piecing Diagram

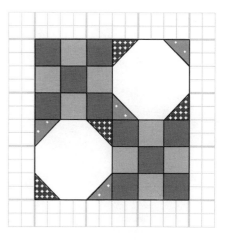

Snowball Unit: Pieces B and C

1. Piece B: Cut 2 squares, each 6½" x 6½". Use Cutoff Template #1, page 20, as a guide to trim off the 4 corners.

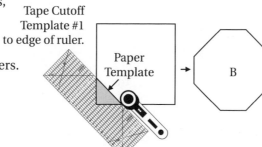

Piece C: Cut 4 squares, each 2⅞" x 2⅞". Layer the squares and cut once diagonally to make 8 half-square triangles.

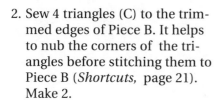

2. Sew 4 triangles (C) to the trimmed edges of Piece B. It helps to nub the corners of the triangles before stitching them to Piece B (*Shortcuts,* page 21). Make 2.

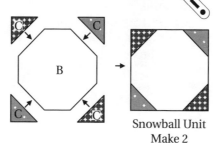

Snowball Unit
Make 2

Snowball Block

Block Assembly

1. Arrange the units as shown in the piecing diagram.
2. Sew the units together in rows.
3. Sew the rows together to complete the block.

JENNY'S BLOCK

Make Jenny's Block to learn how to make a Four Patch unit for the corner and how to make the chevron units for the sides.

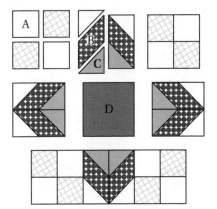

Piecing Diagram

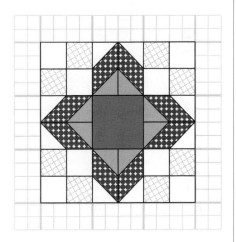

Jenny's Block

Four Patch Corner Units: Piece A

1. Cut 1 strip, 2½" x 22", from Fabric #1 and 1 strip from Fabric #2 (background). (Or, you can use strips left over from previous blocks.)
2. With right sides together and raw edges even, stitch ¼" from one long edge. Press the seam toward the darker fabric.
3. Cut the strip-pieced unit into 8 segments, each 2½" wide.

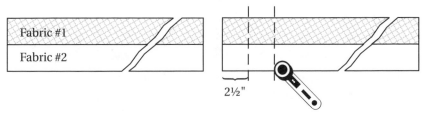

4. Sew 2 segments together to form a Four Patch unit. Make 4 of these units for the block.

Four Patch Unit
Make 4

Chevron Side Units: Pieces B and C

1. Piece B: Cut 1 strip, 2" x 42", for the chevrons. With the strip folded in half as cut, use Chevron Template #2, page 20, to cut a 45° angle (*Shortcuts*, page 18). With the strip still folded, cut 4 sets of chevron units. You will have mirror-image sets of chevron units, one for each side of the block.

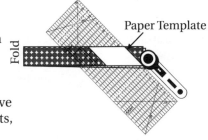

2. Piece C: Cut 4 squares, each 2⅞" x 2⅞", from Fabric #2 and 4 from Fabric #3. Stack the squares and cut once diagonally to yield 16 half-square triangles.
3. Working in pairs, sew a triangle (C) of Fabric #3 to a long edge of each chevron unit (B) as shown. Then sew a triangle (C) of Fabric #2 to the opposite long edge of each chevron unit (C/B).
4. Sew each chevron pair together as shown, carefully matching the seam lines where the chevrons meet.

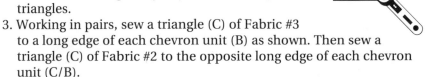

Chevron Pair

Center Unit: Piece D

Cut 1 square, 4½" x 4½".

Block Assembly

1. Arrange the units as shown in the piecing diagram.
2. Sew the units together in horizontal rows.
3. Sew the rows together to complete the block.

Union Square

Make the Union Square Block to learn how to cut and sew half-square and quarter-square triangles. Refer to *Shortcuts*, page 13.

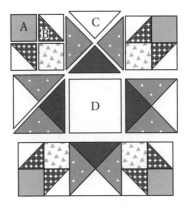

Piecing Diagram

Corner Units: Pieces A and B

1. Piece A: Cut 8 squares, each 2½" x 2½".
2. Piece B: Cut 4 squares, each 2⅞" x 2⅞", from Fabric #1 and 4 from Fabric #2. Layer the squares and cut once diagonally to yield 16 half-square triangles for the corner units.
3. Sew 2 half-square triangles (B), each a different color, together along the bias edges to form a half-square triangle unit. Make 8.

Half-Square Triangle Unit

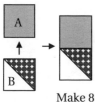 Make 8

4. Sew a square (A) to a half-square triangle unit as shown. Make 8. Then sew 2 of these together to form a Four Patch unit. Make 4.

Make 8   Make 4

Side Units: Piece C

1. Cut 1 square, 5¼" x 5¼", from Fabric #2 and 1 from Fabric #3. Cut 2 squares from Fabric #4. Stack the squares and cut twice diagonally to yield 16 quarter-square triangles.
2. Sew the short sides of 2 triangles (C) together to form a half-square triangle unit. Make 8. Then sew 2 half-square triangle units together to form the side unit. Make 4.

Half-Square Triangle Unit

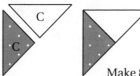

Make 8

Side Unit
Make 4

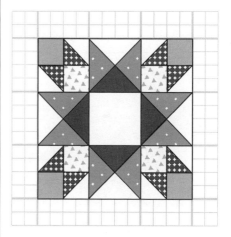

Union Square Block

Center Unit: Piece D

Cut 1 square, 4½" x 4½".

Block Assembly

1. Arrange the units as shown in the piecing diagram.
2. Sew the units together in horizontal rows.
3. Sew the rows together to complete the block.

CARD TRICK

Make the Card Trick Block to learn how to sew half-square units and quarter-square units. Refer to *Shortcuts*, pages 12 and 13. In order for this design to work, you *must* make this block using four different fabrics, plus a background fabric.

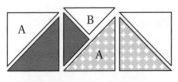

Piecing Diagram

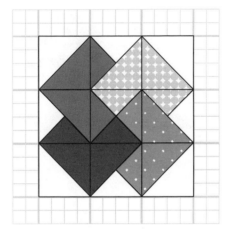

Card Trick Block

Corner Units: Piece A

1. Cut 2 squares, each 4⅞" x 4⅞", from the background fabric.
2. Stack the squares and cut once diagonally to yield 4 half-square triangles for the corners of the block.

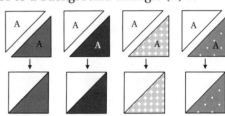

Cards: Piece A

1. From each of the 4 fabrics for the "cards," cut 1 square, 4⅞" x 4⅞".
2. Stack the squares and cut once diagonally as shown above to yield 2 half-square triangles of each color.
3. Sew 1 triangle (A) of each color to a background triangle (A) to form 4 corner units. Press the seam toward the darker fabric. (Use only 1 of each color for the corner units. Set aside the remaining triangles for the side units.)

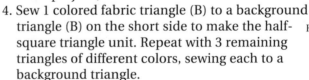

Side Units: Pieces A and B

1. Cut 1 square, 5¼" x 5¼", from the background fabric.
2. From each of the 4 fabrics for the "cards," cut 1 square, 5¼" x 5¼".
3. Stack the squares and cut twice diagonally to yield 4 quarter-square triangles (B) of each color. (Use only 1 of each color to make the side units and 1 of each color for the center unit. Set the extras aside for another project.)
4. Sew 1 colored fabric triangle (B) to a background triangle (B) on the short side to make the half-square triangle unit. Repeat with 3 remaining triangles of different colors, sewing each to a background triangle.

Half-Square Triangle Unit

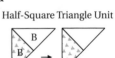

Make 4

5. Sew the half-square triangle unit to triangle (A) left over from the corner units. Color placement is very important in this step. Lay out the block before sewing the units together. Make 4.

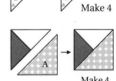

Make 4

Center Unit: Piece B

1. Using the (B) triangles left over from making the side units, sew 2 quarter-square triangles together to make a half-square unit. Again, color placement is very important in this step. Arrange the corner and side units to determine the placement of the quarter-square triangles for the center unit.
2. Sew the half-square units together for the center unit.

Center Unit

Block Assembly

1. Arrange the units as shown in the piecing diagram.
2. Sew the units together in horizontal rows.
3. Sew the rows together to complete the block.

EVENING STAR

Make the Evening Star Block to learn how to sew half-square triangles to quarter-square triangles to make the flying-geese side units.

Corner Units: Piece A

Cut 4 squares, each 3½" x 3½".

Side Units: Pieces B and C

1. Piece B: Cut 1 square, 7¼" x 7¼". Cut twice diagonally to yield 4 quarter-square triangles.

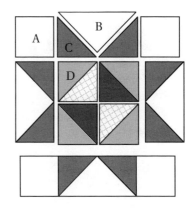

Piecing Diagram

2. Piece C: Cut 4 squares, each 3⅞" x 3⅞". Cut once diagonally to yield 8 half-square triangles.

3. Sew 1 half-square triangle (C) to the short side of the quarter-square triangle (B), then sew another half-square triangle (C) to the other side of the pieced unit. Make 4.

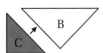

Side Unit
Make 4

Center Unit: Piece D

1. Cut 4 squares, each 3⅞" x 3⅞". Stack the squares and cut once diagonally to yield 8 half-square triangles.

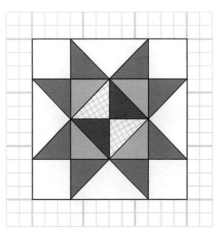

Evening Star Block

2. Sew 2 triangles (D) together on the long side. Make 4.

Make 4

Block Assembly

1. Arrange the units as shown in the piecing diagram.
2. Sew the units together in horizontal rows.
3. Sew the rows together to complete the block.

LAND OF THE MIDNIGHT SUN

Make the Land of the Midnight Sun Block to learn how to modify a half-square triangle to make a trapezoid shape. The color placement in this block is very important.

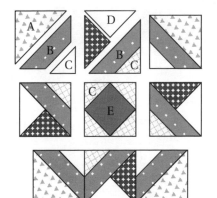

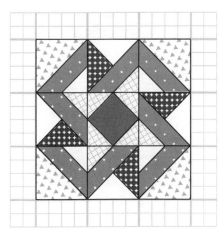

Piecing Diagram

Land of the Midnight Sun Block

Corner Units: Pieces A, B, and C

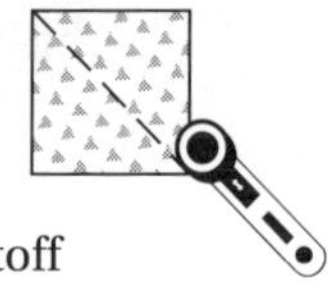

1. Piece A: Cut 2 squares, each 4⅞" x 4⅞". Stack the squares and cut once diagonally to yield 4 half-square triangles.
2. Piece B: Cut 2 squares, each 4⅞" x 4⅞". Stack the squares and cut once diagonally to yield 4 half-square triangles. Use Cutoff Template #1, page 20, to trim off the 90° corner on each one to make a trapezoid shape (*Shortcuts*, page 19).
3. Piece C: Cut 2 squares, each 2⅞" x 2⅞". Cut once diagonally to yield 4 half-square triangles.
4. Sew triangle (C) to trapezoid (B). Press the seam toward the darker fabric. Make 4.
5. Sew a half-square triangle (A) to the pieced unit (C/B). Press the seam toward the darker fabric.

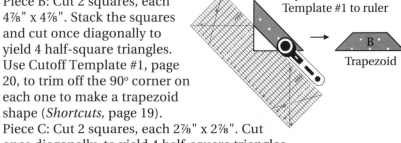

Tape Cutoff Template #1 to ruler

Trapezoid

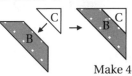

Make 4

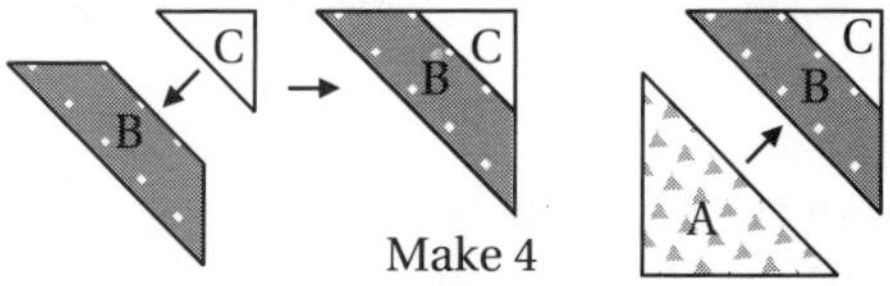

Side Units: Pieces B, C, and D

1. Piece B: Cut 2 squares, each 4⅞" x 4⅞". Stack the squares and cut once diagonally to yield 4 half-square triangles. Use Cutoff Template #1, page 20, to trim off the 90° corners to make a trapezoid shape (*Shortcuts*, page 19).
2. Piece C: Cut 2 squares, each 2⅞" x 2⅞". Cut once diagonally to yield 4 half-square triangles.
3. Piece D: Cut 1 square, 5¼" x 5¼", from Fabric #1 and 1 from Fabric #2. Stack the squares and cut twice diagonally to yield 8 quarter-square triangles.
4. Sew triangles (D) together on the short side. Press the seam toward the darker fabric. Make 4.
5. Sew a triangle (C) to trapezoid (B). Press the seam toward the darker fabric. Sew a triangle unit (D/D), to each pieced unit (C/B). Press the seam toward the trapezoid (B).

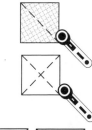

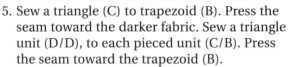

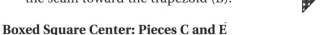

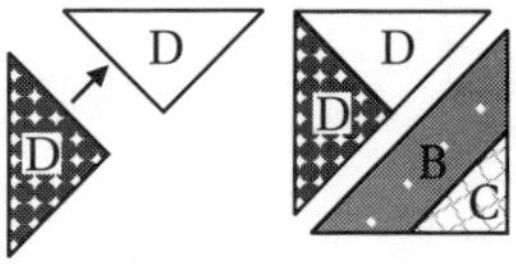

Boxed Square Center: Pieces C and E

1. Piece C: Cut 2 squares, each 2⅞" x 2⅞". Stack the squares and cut once diagonally to yield 4 half-square triangles.
2. Piece E: Cut 1 square, 3⅜" x 3⅜".
3. Sew 2 triangles (C) to opposite corners of square (E). Repeat with the remaining 2 triangles. It helps to nub the corners of the triangles before stitching them to the square (*Shortcuts*, page 21).

Block Assembly

1. Arrange the units as shown in the piecing diagram.
2. Sew the units together in horizontal rows.
3. Sew the rows together to complete the block.

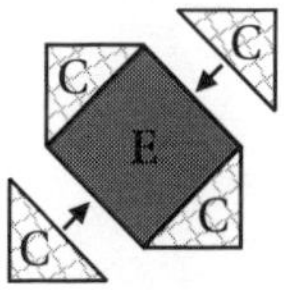

CASTLES IN THE AIR

Make the Castles in the Air Block to learn how to modify a half-square triangle to make a trapezoid.

Corner Units: Pieces A, B, C, and D

1. Piece A: Cut 4 squares, each 2⅞" x 2⅞".
2. Piece B: Cut 2 squares, each 3⅝" x 3⅝", from Fabric #1 and 2 from Fabric #2. Stack the squares and cut twice diagonally to make 16 quarter-square triangles.
3. Sew 2 triangles (B) together on the short side. Make 2 mirror-image units for each corner unit.

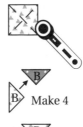
Make 4

Make 4

4. For each corner unit, sew a triangle unit (B/B) to adjacent sides of the square (A). Make 4.

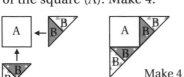
Make 4

5. Piece C: Cut 2 squares, each 5⅝" x 5⅝". Stack the squares and cut once diagonally to yield 4 half-square triangles. Use Cutoff Template #3, page 20, to trim off the 90° corners to make a trapezoid shape (*Shortcuts*, page 19).

Tape Cutoff Template #3 to ruler.

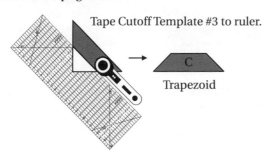

C
Trapezoid

6. Piece D: Cut 2 squares, each 3¼" x 3¼". Stack the squares and cut once diagonally to yield 4 half-square triangles.

7. Sew a triangle (D) to a trapezoid (C) to make a half-square unit. Press seam toward the trapezoid (C). Make 4.

8. Sew a half-square unit (C/D) to a half-square unit (A/B) to complete the corner unit. Make 4.

Side Units: Piece E

1. Cut 1 strip, 3" x 22".
2. Cut the strip into 4 segments, each 3" x 5¼".

Center Unit: Piece F

Cut 1 square, 3" x 3".

Block Assembly

1. Arrange the units as shown in the piecing diagram.
2. Sew the units together in horizontal rows.
3. Sew the rows together to complete the block.

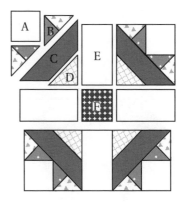
Piecing Diagram

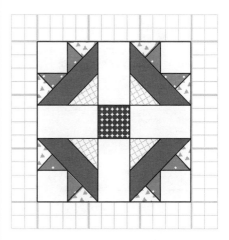
Castles in the Air Block

ROMAN STRIP

Make the Roman Strip Block to learn how to cut a half-square triangle unit from a strip-pieced unit.

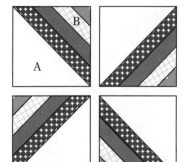

Piecing Diagram

Quarter Block: Pieces A and B

1. Piece A: Cut 2 squares, each 6⅞" x 6⅞". Stack the squares and cut once diagonally to yield 4 half-square triangles.
2. Piece B: From Fabrics #1, #2, and #3, cut 1 strip, 1½" x 42". Cut 1 strip, 2" x 42", from Fabric #4.
3. Sew the strips together in numerical order. Press all seams in one direction.

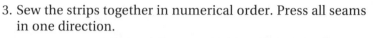

Fabric #1	1½"
Fabric #2	1½"
Fabric #3	1½"
Fabric #4	2"

4. Using the half-square triangle (A) as a template, cut 4 triangles as shown, so that Fabric #4 is always at the point of the triangle. Save the extra triangles in between for another project.

Cut 4, using Piece A as a template.

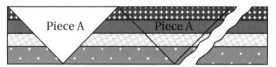

Piece A   Piece A

Not used

5. Sew the strip-pieced half-square triangle (B) to a triangle (A) to make a square. Make 4.

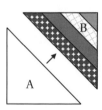

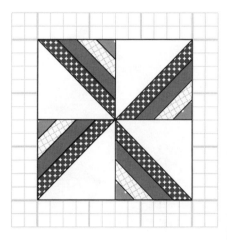

Roman Strip Block

Block Assembly

1. Arrange the squares as shown in the piecing diagram.
2. Sew the squares together in rows.
3. Sew the rows together to complete the block.

FIFTY-FOUR FORTY OR FIGHT

Make the Fifty-Four Forty or Fight Block to learn how to cut and sew half-rectangles. Refer to *Shortcuts,* page 15.

Corner Four Patch Units: Piece A

1. Cut 1 strip, 2½" x 12", from Fabric #1 and Fabric #3; cut 2 strips, each 2½" x 12", from Fabric #2.
2. Sew the strip-piece units as shown. Cut each strip-pieced unit into 4 segments, each 2½" wide.

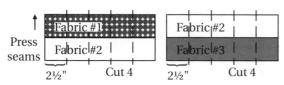

3. Sew 2 segments together to make a Four Patch unit. Make 4.

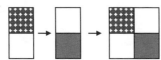

Four Patch Unit
Make 4

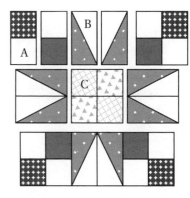

Piecing Diagram

Half-Rectangle Side Units: Piece B

1. Cut 1 strip, 2¾" x 24", from Fabric #3 and 1 from Fabric #4.
2. Cut each strip into 4 rectangles, each 2¾" x 5¼".
3. Cut each rectangle diagonally to make 2 half-rectangles. Trim the points, using Half-Rectangle Template #4, page 20. Transfer the dots on the paper template to the half-rectangles.

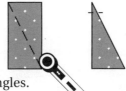

Trim, using Half-Rectangle Template #4.

4. Sew 2 half-rectangles together along the diagonal edge, matching the dots. Press the seam toward the darker fabric. Make 8.

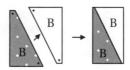

Make 8
Sew half-rectangles together.

5. Sew 2 half-rectangle units together to make the side unit. Make 4.

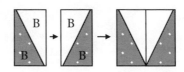

Side Unit
Make 4

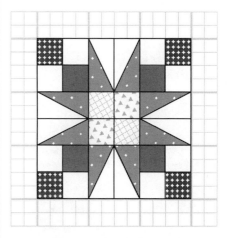

Fifty-Four Forty or Fight Block

Center Four Patch Unit: Piece C

1. Cut 4 squares, each 2½" x 2½".
2. Sew the squares together to form a Four Patch unit.

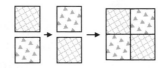

Block Assembly

1. Arrange the units as shown in the piecing diagram.
2. Sew the units together in horizontal rows.
3. Sew the rows together to complete the block.

MORNING STAR

Make the Morning Star Block to learn how to make a pieced diamond cut from a strip-pieced unit. Refer to *Shortcuts*, page 46; however, note that the diamond shown there is made up of nine smaller diamonds. The diamond in this block is made up of four larger diamonds, but the technique is the same. Also learn how to construct an Eight-Pointed Star.

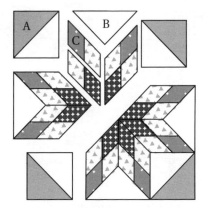

Piecing Diagram (See page 18.)

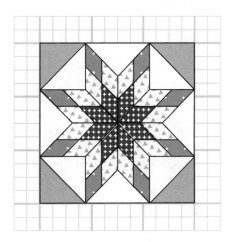

Morning Star Block

Corner Units: Piece A

1. Cut 2 squares, each 4⅜" x 4⅜", from Fabric #1 and 2 from Fabric #2.
2. Stack the squares and cut once diagonally to yield 8 half-square triangles.
3. Sew 2 different fabric triangles (A) together on the long edge. Press the seam toward the darker fabric. Make 4.

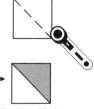

Corner Unit
Make 4

Side Units: Piece B

1. Cut 1 square, 6¼" x 6¼".
2. Cut square twice diagonally to yield 4 quarter-square triangles.

Diamond Units: Piece C

1. Cut 1 strip, 1¾" x 42", from Fabric #3; 2 strips from Fabric #4; and 1 strip from Fabric #5.
2. Sew the Fabric #3 strip to a Fabric #4 strip to make Strip-Pieced Unit #1. Sew the remaining Fabric #4 strip to the Fabric #5 strip to make Strip-Pieced Unit #2.

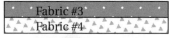
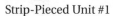
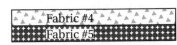

Strip-Pieced Unit #1 · Strip-Pieced Unit #2

3. Place the 2 strip-pieced units next to each other to make sure you cut the correct angle on each strip. At one end of each strip-pieced unit, make a cut at a 45° angle to the long edge.

45° Angle Cut · 45° Angle Cut

4. Cut each strip-pieced unit into 8 segments, each 1¾" wide, making each cut parallel to the previous 45°-angle cut (*Shortcuts*, page 46).

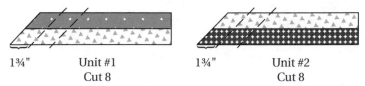

1¾" Unit #1 Cut 8 · 1¾" Unit #2 Cut 8

5. Sew a segment from each strip-pieced unit together to form a diamond. Make 8.

Block Assembly

1. Arrange the units as shown in the piecing diagram.
2. Follow the directions on page 18 for construction of the Eight-Pointed Star to assemble this block.

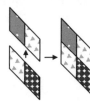

Make 8

STAR OF THE EAST

Make the Star of the East Block to learn how to cut a half-length diamond from a strip-pieced unit. Refer to *Shortcuts*, pages 44 and 45.

Corner Units: Piece A

Cut 4 squares, each 4" x 4".

Side Units: Piece B

1. Cut 1 square, 6¼ x 6¼".
2. Cut the square twice diagonally to yield 4 quarter-square triangles.

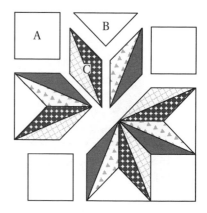

Piecing Diagram (See page 18.)

Half-Length Pieced Diamond Units: Piece C

1. Cut 1 strip, 2" x 42", from Fabric #1, Fabric #2, Fabric #3, and Fabric #4.
2. Sew Fabric #1 and Fabric #2, right sides together. Stitch the strips ¼" from both long edges. Do the same for Fabric #3 and Fabric #4. Use Strip Star Template #5, page 20, to cut 4 triangles from each strip-pieced unit (*Shortcuts*, page 44).

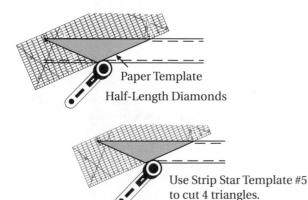

Paper Template
Half-Length Diamonds

Use Strip Star Template #5
to cut 4 triangles.

Turn cut piece over. Align template with first cut
edge and trim up second side.

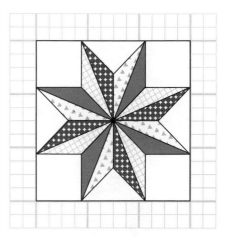

Star of the East Block

3. Carefully undo the stitching at the point of each piece, open out into a diamond, and press the seam open.

 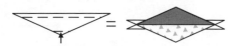

Half-Length
Pieced Diamond

Remove stitches at point
and press diamond open.

Block Assembly

1. Arrange the units as shown in the piecing diagram.
2. Follow the directions on page 18 for construction of the Eight-Pointed Star to assemble this block.

HOW TO CONSTRUCT AN EIGHT-POINTED (LE MOYNE) STAR

The simplest way to construct a Le Moyne Star is to attach the background pieces to the diamond-shaped star pieces first and then sew the star pieces to each other. As you sew the pieces together, you will notice that the seams must turn a corner where the background pieces meet the star pieces. To do this accurately, you must stop stitching *exactly* ¼" from the raw edge at the end of each seam where the pieces meet.

Piecing the diamond unit

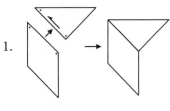

1.

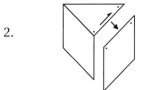

2.

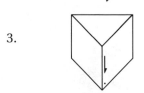

3.

Adding a square

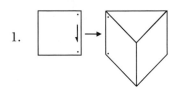

1.

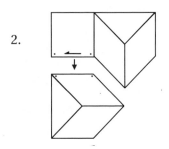

2.

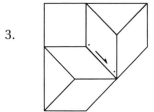

3.

To make the diamond units, each made up of 2 diamonds and 1 triangle:
1. Sew the triangle to a diamond. Begin stitching exactly ¼" from the inner edge of the 2 pieces. Stitch all the way to the outer edge of the block.
2. Sew a second diamond to the triangle, starting at the inner point exactly ¼" from the raw edges. Stitch to the outer edge of the block.
3. Match the points of the diamonds and sew them together. Press this seam to one side and press the triangle seams toward the diamonds.

To add a square between 2 diamond units:
1. Sew a square to the diamond unit. Start sewing on the outer edge and end your stitching ¼" from the inner edge.
2. Sew the second diamond unit to the square. Begin stitching ¼" from the inner point and stitch to the outer edge.
3. Match the points of the diamonds and sew them together; press the seam in one direction. Press the seams between the square and diamond units toward the diamonds.

To join the 2 units with the remaining squares:
1. Sew edges of the diamond units to both edges of 1 square.
2. Repeat with the remaining square.

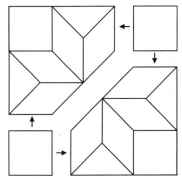

Sew center seam last.

To assemble the block:
1. Match the center points and pin.
2. Pull the corner squares out of the way and stitch.
3. Press the center seam to one side and press the seams of the squares toward the diamonds.

SETTING THE BLOCKS

Lattice Units
1. Cut 26 strips, each 1¼" x 42", from dark fabric. Cut 13 strips, each 2½" x 42", from background fabric.
2. Make 13 strip-pieced lattice units as shown. From the strip-pieced units, cut 31 segments, each 12½" wide, for the lattices. Cut 20 segments, each 2½" wide, and set aside for the cornerstone units.

Cornerstone Units
1. Cut 4 strips, each 1¼" x 42", from contrasting fabric. Cut 2 strips, each 2½" x 42", from dark fabric. Make 2 strip-pieced units as shown. Cut 40 segments, each 1¼" wide, from the strip-pieced units.
2. Assemble cornerstones as shown, using the 1¼"-wide segments just cut and the 2½"-wide segments set aside earlier. Make 20.

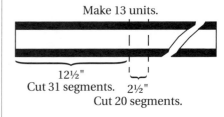

Make 13 units.

12½"
Cut 31 segments. 2½"
Cut 20 segments.

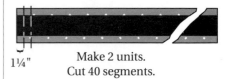

1¼"

Make 2 units.
Cut 40 segments.

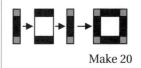

Make 20

QUILT TOP ASSEMBLY

1. Referring to the quilt plan on page 5, arrange the blocks in rows of 3 across and 4 down, with lattice strips between the blocks and at the outer edges of each row. Place blocks in an arrangement that pleases you.
2. Sew blocks and lattices together in horizontal rows. Make 4 rows.

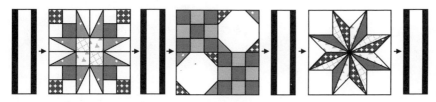

Make 4 rows.

3. Make 5 rows of alternating cornerstones and lattices, beginning and ending with a cornerstone in each row.

Make 5 rows.

4. Sew cornerstone/lattice to blocks as shown in quilt plan, page 5.

BORDERS

1. From the border fabric, cut 2 strips, each 4½" x 60", for the top and bottom. Cut 2 strips, each 4½" x 76", for the sides. Sew the border strips to the quilt, with 4½" of each strip extending beyond the raw edges of the quilt at each end for mitering corners.
2. Place 1 corner of the quilt on the ironing board, right side up, and pin in place. Fold under 1 strip at a 45° angle; pin and press. Center a strip of 1"-wide masking tape over the mitered fold, removing pins as you go. Remove quilt from ironing board.
3. On the wrong side, fold the quilt as shown and draw a stitching line on the border. Stitch on the line and remove the masking tape from the right side. Trim away any excess border, leaving a ¼"-wide seam allowance beyond the stitching. Press the seam open. Repeat with remaining corners.

QUILT FINISHING

1. Layer the completed quilt top with batting and backing; baste.
2. Quilt as desired.
3. Bind the edges of the quilt.

1. Sew border to quilt.

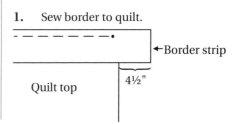

←Border strip

Quilt top   4½"

2. Press fold under   Tape

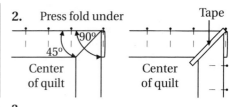

90°
45°
Center of quilt   Center of quilt

3.

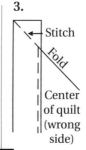

← Stitch
Fold
Center of quilt (wrong side)

TEMPLATES

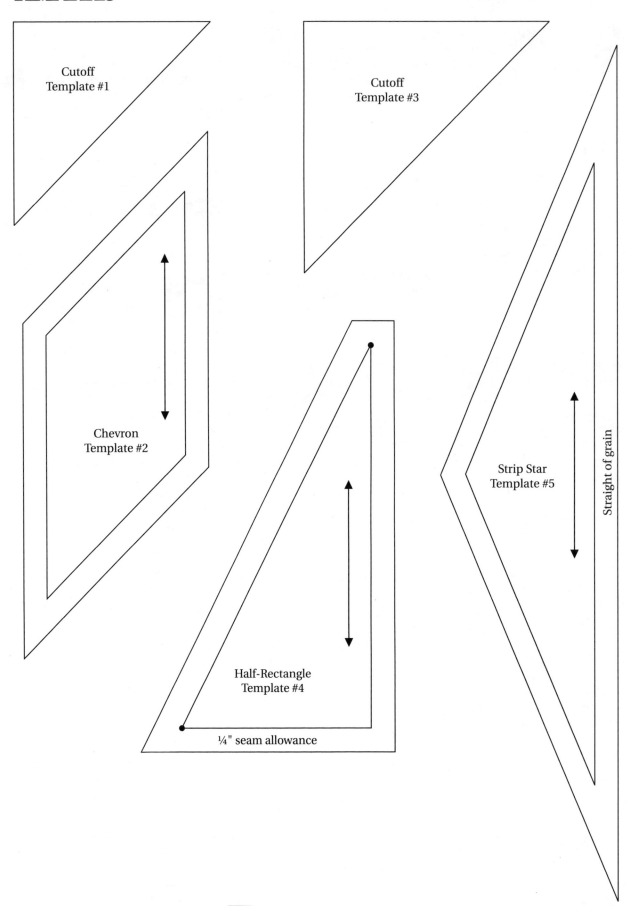

Cutoff
Template #1

Cutoff
Template #3

Chevron
Template #2

Half-Rectangle
Template #4

¼" seam allowance

Strip Star
Template #5

Straight of grain